TEETH NEVER SLEEP

CANTO MUNDO
POETRY SERIES
EDITED BY DEBORAH PAREDEZ
AND CELESTE MENDOZA

Other Titles in This Series

Jacob Shores-Argüello | *Paraíso*

TEETH NEVER SLEEP

POEMS BY
ÁNGEL GARCÍA

The University of Arkansas Press
Fayetteville
2018

Copyright © 2018 by The University of Arkansas Press
All rights reserved
Manufactured in the United States of America

ISBN: 978-1-68226-073-9
e-ISBN: 978-1-61075-647-1

22 21 20 19 18   5 4 3 2 1

Designed by Liz Lester

♾ The paper used in this publication meets the minimum requirements of the American National Standard for Permanence of Paper for Printed Library Materials Z39.48-1984.

Library of Congress Control Cataloging-in-Publication Data

Names: García, Ángel, 1981–   author.
Title: Teeth never sleep : poems / by Ángel García.
Description: Fayetteville : University of Arkansas Press, 2018. | Series: CantoMundo Poetry Prize Series | Includes bibliographical references.
Identifiers: LCCN 2018003961 | ISBN 9781682260739 (softcover : acid-free paper)
Classification: LCC PS3607.A69 A6 2018 | DDC 811/.6—dc23
LC record available at https://urldefense.proofpoint.com/v2/url?u=https-3A__lccn.loc.gov_2018003961&d=DwIFAg&c=7ypwAowFJ8v-mw8AB-SdSueVQgSDL4HiiSaLK01W8HA&r=4fo1OqKuv_3krqlYYqNQWNKNaWxXN20G1PCOL-2ERgE&m=1wA5EqUFSKMyiY0LrJ2DjY5rPvLM8lCXbcq3t2Jx-V4&s=fGPmm1JiFYu19KDCPHgpSY8V5Tlirpr9-rO9F6x7Ulw&e=

This book is dedicated to my brothers, who showed me how to be a better man; to my father and mother who made everything possible. I hope these pages inspire us to share our untold stories.

Inch by inch I conquered the inner terrain
I was born with. Bit by bit I reclaimed
the swamp in which I'd languished. I gave
birth to my infinite being, but I had to
wrench myself out of me with forceps.

—*Fernando Pessoa*

SERIES EDITORS' PREFACE

"You've come here because / for too many years you've carried a fiery ember / that finally, in a field of cane, will flame into dawn." So burn these meditations on violence and Latino masculinity that light up Ángel García's narrative lyrics and prose poems. Throughout the book, García refuses to shy away from difficult and sometimes bloody outbursts and expressions of masculine rage. He takes the reader through every *rinconcito* of a man who experiences his masculinity as a struggle between the beast that "doesn't / have a name and runs wild" and the man who tries to live without drowning inside this beast, "the one inside you, you are unable to tame."

These are poems that unflinchingly interrogate the formations and deformations of manhood. "From my father's belly," García writes, "I'm spit out—horned, hooved and / halved." His work reaches back to the ghastly and ghostly origins of misogyny that are embedded in and passed down through familial relations and cultural myths—from the legend of La Llorona to the lingering presence of absent fathers. Here, fantastical beasts converse and converge with everyday beasts in language that is searing and stripped of sentimentality. García's work offers a timely and rigorous excavation of the sources and forces of Latino machismo and of masculinity writ large, and as such, is a fitting recipient of the second annual CantoMundo Poetry Prize.

Since our founding in 2009 by a collective of cross-generational Latinx poets—Norma E. Cantú, Celeste Guzman Mendoza, Pablo Miguel Martínez, Deborah Paredez, and Carmen Tafolla—CantoMundo has sought to provide a space for the creation of Latinx poetry and a community of support for Latina/o poets. Central to CantoMundo's mission is desire to create opportunities—both within and beyond established institutions—for the development, documentation, performance, and publication of Latinx poetry: a *canto-mundo*, a world of song, sustained by the wide-ranging voices of Latinx poets.

The CantoMundo Poetry Series arises out of CantoMundo's efforts to support and showcase Latinx poets from across the linguistic, aesthetic, stylistic, and cultural spectrums in which they write. The series values the traditions and communities from which contemporary Latinx poets emerge while also encouraging an engagement with innovative Latinx aesthetics and poetics.

Teeth Never Sleep combines the Latinx poetic and philosophical traditions of Gloria Anzaldúa and Andrés Montoya with the original and daring visions of a new generation of Latinx poets. García's poems ruminate on the burdens and borders of embodiment, ultimately offering up "a tooth   a bone   a ballad." About García's collection, this year's guest judge, Rafael Campo, observes:

> Sometimes ferocious, and always ferociously honest, Ángel García's poems address themselves to the cycle of violence that arises at the many borders, both enforced and inhabited, in the US Latino experience: between macho stereotypes and sensuous masculinity, between painful alienation and penitent acceptance, and ultimately, between loss and love. Yet for all the bruised fists, black eyes, and broken jaws here, there are no victims in these harrowing poems, as they search not for blame, but for bravery—the courage to see oneself in the mirror, and recognize our universal humanity always hungrily staring back.

The speaker in García's poems interrogates the beastliness of toxic masculinity not as a self-congratulatory display of contrition nor as simply a plea for penance. Nowhere do these poems fall prey to easy absolution. For these reasons, García's work is of great urgency during this historic moment marked by the revelations of long-entrenched practices of sexual violence in every *rinconcito* of our society. *Teeth Never Sleep* exposes and disarms the various phases of manhood—from boyhood to fatherhood—taking aim at patriarchy with fierce precision like a cobra extending its hood as it strikes.

Celeste Mendoza and Deborah Paredez

ACKNOWLEDGMENTS

I am grateful to the editors of the following publications in which these poems, some of them in earlier versions, have appeared.

The Acentos Review: "La Llorona's Husband Foresees His Own Death" & "La Llorona's Husband Experiences Anger" & "La Llorona's Husband Sleepwalks"

The American Poetry Review: "Spanish Midterm" & "Conversations with My Father"

Askew Poetry Journal: "Teeth Never Sleep II"

The Boiler Journal: "Antipode II" & "Stampede"

Connotation Press: "Falling Asleep" & "Morning Breath" & "Coming Home"

DecomP magazine: "Meditations on Leaving"

Huizache: "Full Moon" & "Portraits of Beasts: Nombre"

Into the Teeth of the Wind: "Teeth Never Sleep"

Miramar: "Broke" & "Bones" & "Quaker Oats" & "Elegy for What Once Slept in a Cage"

Packinghouse Review: "Ash"

RHINO: "Self-Portraits of a Man as Beast: Coward"

San Pedro River Review: "Antipode"

Spillway—A Poetry Magazine: "Blood" & "Alebrije"

Tinderbox: "Portraits of Beasts: Unarmed" & "I Smoke My Last Cigarette While Andres Montoya Preaches to the Willow Tree"

Many thanks to the founders of CantoMundo and my fellow CantoMundistas; the founders of the Community of Writers—Squaw Valley; and the Vermont Studio Center and the sponsors of the Lukas Riveros Amani Fellowship who have all so generously provided me with community and continued support. For their unwavering belief and mentorship when I needed it most, I would like to thank Jesus Solano, Matais Pouncil, Cindy Cruz, liz Gonzalez, and Verónica Reyes. For their guidance and crucial instruction: Frank Gaspar, David Dominguez, Janét Hund, Ralph Angel, Joy Manesiotis, Eliza Rodriguez y Gibson, Leela MadhavaRau, Christopher Buckley, Juan Felipe Herrera, Chris Abani, Grace Bauer, Ted Kooser, Kwame Dawes, and Amelia María de la Luz Montes. To the fellow poets who've helped shape this manuscript over the years: Xochitl-Julisa Bermejo, Sara Borjas, Anthony Cody, Rachelle Cruz, Leticia Hernández-Linares, DaMaris Hill, Katie Pryor, Luivette Resto, and Chet'la Sebree—I am grateful for your friendship and generosity. To Javier Calderon and Jesus Sanchez—thank you for your brotherhood. A special thanks to Rafael Campo, Deborah Paredez, and Celeste Guzmán Mendoza for making this book possible. Thank you to David Scott Cunningham, Molly Bess Rector, Melissa King, Charlie Shields, and everyone else at the University of Arkansas Press. And finally, to Janett Barragan Miranda, who lovingly helped shape many of these poems and who has given me more than I could ever ask for.

CONTENTS

El Esposo de la Llorona Habla   3

I

Broke   7
Antipode II   9
El Esposo de la Llorona Prevé su Propia Muerte   10
Bones   11
Teeth Never Sleep   12
Dinner Time   13
El Esposo de la Llorona Enfrenta Ira   14
Rinconcito   15
Exuviae   16
Piss   17
El Esposo de la Llorona Encuentra Negación   20
A Dog Poem   21
Stampede   22

II

Self-Portraits of a Man as Beast   25
    Coward   25
    Freeway Exits   26
    Chingarla   27
    Ablutions   28
    Hunger   29
    Giving It   30
    Nombre   31

III Lobe 35
Ash 36
El Esposo de la Llorona Negocia 38
Blood 39
Meditations on Leaving 40
Spanish Midterm 44
Elegy for What Once Slept in a Cage 46
El Esposo de la Llorona Habla a los Muertos 53
Conversations with My Father 54
Domestic Dispute 56
El Esposo de la Llorona Reza 57
Falling Asleep 58

IV Portraits of Beasts 61
    Alebrije 61
    Strange and Worried Animal 62
    Hombre-Lobo 63
    Cannibal 65
    Filicide 66
    Suspect 67
    Opossum 68

V Morning Breath 71
El Esposo de La Llorona Visita la Tumba de su Madre 72
Coming Home 73
Quaker Oats 74
Teeth Never Sleep II 75
El Esposo de La Llorona se Encuentra Solo 76
Full Moon 77

I Smoke My Last Cigarette While Andrés Montoya
Preaches to the Willow Tree   79

El Esposo de La Llorona Tiene una Mirada de Esperanza   81

Antipode   82

Cages   83

Meditations on Loss   84

Notes   89

TEETH NEVER SLEEP

EL ESPOSO DE LA LLORONA HABLA

Estas palabras no son mías
a tooth   a bone   a ballad
sung by the dead   nightly
I feed them   nectar
dress   their wounds
these things   I've harmed
because I   can't stand
to watch   what bleeds
I drown   my hands
each night   I light candles
to block   the nightmares
that flap   their wings
against   my window
there is   only
one   creature
left   to forgive

I

BROKE

Woken up by the roach between my toes, I promise
the woman beside me something better, something
beyond thin walls through which we listen to neighbors
making love in the next apartment, their loud pleas

to a god whose name we never spoke out loud. Or
the cries of lovers crossed, promising that this will
be the last night of chaos, the last night of arguing
over the lost rent or the last promise of the last drink

in a bar where promises sit on stools, lost and drunk.
And what lies hidden in my sock drawer, tongue-tied,
is all I'm capable of. Nothing more. Each night I lock
the door and turn the deadbolt, knowing what we're

unsafe from is a lifetime of loving one another poorly.
And it's not the notes past due stacked in a shoebox
like love letters or the empty fridge grumbling that are
my failure. In the gray mornings of new days, shades

drawn, I search the room for my boots and worn shirt,
black-stained and sweaty. Seconds before I walk out
the door, I watch her on our bed, the warm-bread scent
of her body filling the room. I take off my work clothes

to lie down beside her and feel the creature between us,
its breath ragged and difficult—not a child, but a shadow,
a space growing between us, wider and deeper because
what little we have left, we've worked too hard for.

Still, I'm too weak for solitude. I can't afford it.
In the coming light, I close my eyes and hope
the truth I'll never reveal—that I am broke, that
together we are broken—will scurry into the dark.

ANTIPODE II

Miles from here, in a field of cane there hangs
the scarecrow that resembles so closely a man
it could be mistaken for your father. Or no one.
The helmsman, who crosses you for pesos, asks
why have you come back here? As always, you
have no answers. Only a vague memory of your
father swinging a machete through the wild stalks
to place on your tongue the first sweet thing you
tasted. Nothing is like it used to be. The river is
so still now it looks as if the world's upside down.
You've come here dragging that towrope from
city to city with nowhere to anchor, a rancid taste
in your mouth. Admit it. You're no better a man
than your father. You've come here because
for too many years you've carried a fiery ember
that finally, in a field of cane, will flame into dawn.

EL ESPOSO DE LA LLORONA
PREVÉ SU PROPIA MUERTE

After the rain: the small scatter of death.
A boy cries near the muddy bank, his

hair damp river moss, worms wriggling
over his bare feet. His voice is a stream.

Eyes clouded oil stains floating over
shallow puddles, he reaches out for me.

I want to embrace his blue and bloated body,
run my fingers across his moonlit scales.

He screeches toward me, swallows me
whole. Pulls my bones from his mouth,

spits out my teeth, one by one, into this
river pregnant with flesh, wet with skin.

BONES

I've searched in river bottoms,
trudged through the mud, silt-
blind, and tight-lipped, mumbled
beneath my breath. My tongue:
a leech suckling from the heart
in my mouth. A poem. The first
and last words. Always. Father. Fa-
ther. Teetering on the tip of my
tongue. Father. Father. Because
you don't speak ill of the dead.
Father. Father. Because you do
not speak ill of the still-living
but long-departed. Father. Fa-
ther. All my dark words, bone
dry and sickly. Father. Father.
Words falling farther, further,
deeper into my mouth, my throat
a casket closed and rusted shut.

TEETH NEVER SLEEP

they sing, inside the pillow of your mouth,
the same sad song—tooth ground against
tooth—a music made crudely from bones.

What spills from your lips into your palm
—blood puddled—are all the words you've
swallowed: a constant quiet, dying of hunger.

DINNER TIME

Doors are not to be slammed in this house, but closed, gently. The click of a door latch before each room takes a last breath. At the table, I sit in front of a massive feast. It is only us three: what's left of a family: my father, my mother, and I, each of us breathing slowly in our seats while I pass the minutes before bed, starving for a glance. My father sits, hands clutching fork and knife, his jaw pulsing as he devours every morsel on his plate. My mother stares off. Not through the dining room window, not at family photos nailed to the wall, but at the wall itself. I spread mounds of food shoveled before me across my plate, hunched over in my chair, holding, in my left hand, my fork. *Sit close to the table. Finish everything on your plate. Sit up straight.* Neither one reprimands. When they push away from the table to their separate rooms, I clear away the leftovers I'll eat later, alone in my room, with my door closed. In the kitchen, over the sink, I wash each utensil, scrub each glass and plate, careful not to drop, nick, crack, or smash a single dish.

EL ESPOSO DE LA LLORONA ENFRENTA IRA

I'll break you. I'll break you. I'll break you. For good measure, break you again. Break lip. Break nose. Break both cheekbones. Break you until you are an open wound, breathing. Threaten more breaking when the breaking is done. Later, I'll pick up, shard by shard, what's left of your broken name. Put you together again—in pieces. When you leave, or try to, I will break you. Break you, again. Always, my broken love.

RINCONCITO

to the world I cried out loud—*fucking racist pig*—
before being pushed into the back seat of a cruiser,
arms creased behind me, wrists cuffed and bleeding

    voy a buscar un rinconcito en el cielo para llevar a mi amor

hunched over in the dark corner of a drunk tank,
I crossed my arms over my knees to try and sleep,
ninety degrees of concrete the only thing holding me up

    voy a buscar un rinconcito en el cielo para escondernos tú y yo

released, my shadow tucked between my legs, I
crossed Anaheim and heard a man on the corner
sing in Spanish the only song I know about heaven

    un rinconcito en el cielo, juntos unidos los dos

at home we caved into each other as I cried out
for forgiveness, *I love you, I really love you,* the taste
in my mouth still sour from too much beer

    y cuando caiga la noche te daré mi amor

sleeping head to feet in a twin bed too small for
our bodies, we woke up and made love. *Come in me,*
you said, and I did: because I had nothing left to give

EXUVIAE

I enter my dorm room and hang myself
from a door hook: sweat-stained t-shirt,
belt buckle and pants, socks tucked inside
the quietest of tongues. There is always
order to undressing before a new lover.
The sucked gut, the tug of crown and testes
before turning around, the deliberate steps
to the bed where I crawl toward her body.
All mouth. And empty. Neck, nipple, navel.
Lobe, lip, labia. Order. Order. Order. Until
my cell vibrates on the bed stand when I enter
her. The two a.m. knock on the door as I'm about
to come. My girlfriend calling out my name
from the dark hallway. The shell of me, hung
from a metal hook behind the door, trembling.

PISS

I'm standing before a urinal in a room full of urinals—
hundreds, white-toothed and impeccable, a porcelain
simper mocking the baby chick in my hands. I freeze,
though my boy body is ready: the sudden shudder
of goose flesh, the release and trickle, a stream the color
of too little water to drink. Warmth rising. But when it
comes, it comes clumsily and full of consequences: drops
of urine spotting my pant legs and shoes, speckling my
hands, pee pouring down my thigh, my knee, then foot,
drowning, drowning, in what tastes like the sea, salt water
and toxin, the bladder's dirty bath water, a weak stream
now a river, a deafening cascade that sweeps me awake.

～

What pools on the mattress
                        becomes darker than the night.
Startled, body shivering, I lie
                        still and understand the cold
crawling across my body
                        is something bad I've done.
In the bathroom, I undress
                        in the dark. Ball up my clothes
inside the balled-up sheets
                        and sneak outside to the trash.

～

Because nothing would stop my father from getting where
he wanted to go, on hours-long road trips, we knew to ask
for nothing—not food if we were hungry, not something
to drink, not one five-minute stop so we could all take
a piss on the side of the road. Instead, we saved two-liter
bottles and took turns, four boys—my brothers and I—kneeling
in the back of the van, each of us trying to steady our aim,
maintain balance. My shorts barely covered my ass as I tried
to stick the worm between my legs into the mouth of the bottle—
making the occasional spill, warm urine running down my hands,
trailing over my fingers, crying over the bottle, unable
to control my body, angry at another ritual failure.

~

My father picks me up for the weekend.

not true

He tells me he's missed me since leaving.

not true

He pulls up along the curb and says, *we're here*.

not true

Not a home, but a curb painted red.

not true

A van parked along the street.

not true

The acrid scent of his tools, dizzying.

not true

Wrench, hammer, screwdriver, nails.

not true

I ask him, where do you go to the bathroom?

not true

Two-liter bottles lined up in the back of the van.

not true

Some empty. Some full.

not true

I am thirteen the first time I pity my father.

true

~

In the van, I lie beside my father while he sleeps.
A street lamp bathes us in light; the constant hum
makes it impossible for me to fall asleep. Instead,
I watch the shadows of homeless men peer into
the windows. Hours before I have to get up for
school, I tell myself I can hold it, that I'm too old
to piss myself. I watch a cop slip a ticket beneath
the wiper blade, watch it wrinkle with the morning
dew, imagine the familiar *goddammit* escaping his lips,
hoping that maybe this is what'll make him angry
—not the urine spreading over my belly as I watch,
in shame, the morning sun turn the sky liquid.

EL ESPOSO DE LA LLORONA
ENCUENTRA NEGACIÓN

The hushed tongue writhing in my hand will soon die.
If I never say the names of the dead, they'll live forever.

A DOG POEM

This is the poem I've always wanted to write about a dog, a puppy really, a small puppy who followed me to the beach one day in Ensenada when I was just a boy, about how we played on that beach, how happy I was, both of us, really, running in the sand, playing in the ripples of ocean; it's about the smell of his wet fur, so salty, pressed against my nose as I dried him with my shirt; it's about our walk home, the game I played tiptoeing on the curb, my arms flung out as if in flight, trying not to fall, and the dog behind me, trotting along in the street trying to keep up; it's about the van that drove by and did not stop, the yelp from beneath the wheel; it's about his flattened body, the way his innards pushed out from his mouth—his lungs, his heart lying there on the concrete road; it's about the last breaths he took, the puddle of blood that pooled beneath him, the way his small body twitched and finally went still; about how I cried on the walk back, alone, and believed that it was my fault for not paying attention, for walking too quickly, for not somehow stopping the van; it's about getting home and telling no one, saying nothing about the dog I got killed.

STAMPEDE

You don't know this horse.
What you love most doesn't
have a name and runs wild.
Ridden with guilt, you slept
in a field, naked and hungry,
committed to memory the cold:
how it sunk its teeth into your
body one mouthful at a time.
That night all the small animals
you'd buried came alive. You
told yourself, *don't be afraid.*
I am no longer that man. Laid
your head on the dirt and watched
the grass trill, heard the beating
in your chest for the first time:
the beasts starting to stampede.

II

SELF-PORTRAITS OF A MAN AS BEAST

Coward

Finally. Someone says it. I wonder if I'm ready to turn around and face it—this moment, this minute—I've been waiting for half my life when I first realize the weight of my hands clenched in a ball is more capable than hands stuffed in my pocket, always fumbling for change that might, finally, be enough to take me away from everything I've known: this crowded bar, the darkened streets, the woman I pretended to love in high school—the first of many I entered whispering what I knew was a lie. This may be too much for me, a man who doesn't know about tomorrow, or the next town, or the life I'll live if now, tonight, broke in a bar, I don't turn around to face this shadow, or voice, or maybe no one at all—just the chairs already hanging from their tables, the jukebox unplugged—only me and a congregation of moths circling the light bulbs, which just now have been shut off.

Freeway Exits

To avoid the click of the seatbelt unbuckling so the one driving doesn't notice: I raise the volume, throw from the now-open window the last bottle I've drunk. I've stopped counting how many more off-ramps until we exit. I don't want to go home. The freeway lights pass in a haze. Seventy-five mph. Something, voice slurred and stupid, says: *Open the door. Jump out.* Inside, the dome light shines. The woman I love mouths my name. Screams, *No*. Passing beneath me are dark waters. The woman driving screams she loves me—something I know but can't bear to hear.

Chingarla

Men who knew her and loved her longer circle to tell me in Spanish, beer cans in our hands, empties kicked between our unsteady stances: *put your foot down.*

The sun sets blood orange. Birds flock in a far-off field over something dead. *Look how your woman is disrespecting you.* I watch her dance too closely with another man, song after song after song.

Next morning, on the two-and-a-half-hour drive home, she lay curled in the back seat. I watched her, from the rearview mirror, grow smaller and smaller.

Ablutions

"Devoted son. Macho pig."

Sunday morning, slowly, my entire body hungover and sore, I begin to clean the way my mother taught me—top to bottom, ceiling to floor—*Because*, she said, *I don't want you to depend on a woman.* Even now, with a warm-damp washcloth wrapped around a broomstick I clean first the places I'm unable to reach. Then the walls, to wash away their secrets. Counter tops dusted. Stove degreased and scrubbed. Bleach in the sink to help swallow what's been unswallowed. I pick up bottles and cans from the floor, the cigarette butts from their makeshift trays. Vacuum and sweep what's left of yesterday. This is what I've taught myself: how to wash away blood. One tablespoon of soap for the spots. One tablespoon ammonia for the pools still bleeding. This is the way I love a woman. I go back to the bedroom and crawl in beside her, my lover, still sleeping in the dark. I tell her, *I've cleaned the house so you can sleep in.* My hands still stained in the blush of her cheek.

Hunger

All over a cheeseburger, she says. We both laugh, still drunk in bed. My face hurts from the beating I've been given by another man.

At a Jack in the Box drive-thru I exit the car and beg him to hurt me. This is the only way I want to be touched: his fists pummeling my face. I get back up from each fall, asking for seconds and thirds.

On the way home, I catch my reflection in the side view mirror and begin to cry. My face swollen and bruised, I am unrecognizable.

Giving It

I don't remember the knuckles' attempt to shatter her cheekbone. I remember only what's left the next morning: shards of glass beneath the now-empty window frame; the small, black halos of cigarette butts burned into our bed; my fingerprints etched purple into her thin wrists; her cheek bruised in blues. The word piruja perched on my lips. Shades drawn, we speak in shadows of what, last night, happened in shadows. In the dark, I hear only her voice trembling. *You hit me and when I tried to leave you, you hit me more.* I try to piece memory together, make sense of what's blacked out. Again, I fail. Then that feeling. It's hard for me to breathe. I say her name softly, as if learning it for the first time. When we make love, because we always make love, I apologize for everything I don't remember doing, everything I never remember saying. Hating, always, the moment when I'll turn on the light.

Nombre

My name breaks into a two-bedroom house where ghosts live. The doormat reads, *Home is Heaven*. My name likes the idea of this. It breaks in. It robs. Gets caught. Does time. In a cell. Six by eight. Where all you own is your name. Recently found dead. On the floor. My name is what happens when you're afraid to be free, a secret said so softly in your ear, you'll ask again *what was his name?* My name sometimes forgets its name, calls itself *nombre* instead. Un hombre. There are no angels here. There are no angels here. Just a name who can't forgive his father, who can't forgive his own sins. My name watches over me at night. Or drags me from my bed, burning.

LOBE

We lie in bed when she tells me she is pregnant. I imagine a body, tender and small, the lobe of an ear floating in her belly. Already, I am eager to whisper a name.

Ángel, she says, *I'm not ready to have a baby*. I rise and sit on the edge of our bed, cover my face with my hands. Still, a part of me believes a man shouldn't cry in front of a woman, even in the dark.

She sits beside me and searches for my face. Gently, she peels my hands away, finger after finger. She places her hands in mine. Our small embrace, warm, wet, and empty.

ASH

Children who know nothing of snow
dig in their thin pockets for change
to ask the woman pushing a shopping cart
for a raspado: her raspador scraping over
a block of ice, the already-melting mound
pushed into the mouth of a Styrofoam cup,
each crystal as white as the clouds passing
above. When they sit on the stoop to slurp
the sweetness their lips reveal everything
about want: limes hanging from a backyard
limb, strawberries bleeding on the kitchen
table, the blue of the stringy sky—nothing
is as it seems. Today, the sky is filled with
soot and most of California is burning. What
falls from the sky and piles onto the parked
cars is something *like* snow. Only there are
no children outside to roll snowmen, to lie
down on the lawn, coats growing wet as they
form angels, to pack snowballs tightly into fists.
                              Everything quiet.
I sit on the porch beside my girlfriend
watching ash fall and cover the city in gray.
She has lived on this block all her life and has
never seen snow. The first time I saw it fall
I was only five, living in Texas. I begged
my mother to let me outside, and after

she wrapped me in coat after coat I went out.
I tell my girlfriend I did not play—convinced
snow was some kind of miracle— tell her
how I knelt down to carefully scoop several
handfuls of snow into my eager mouth, and how
my tongue, for the rest of the day, kept burning.

EL ESPOSO DE LA LLORONA NEGOCIA

For years, I believed the myth. If not god,
at least the son of god. I am nothing, no one:

not water turned to wine turned to blood.
Only flesh. Only the marrow in my bones.

From the disintegrating temple of my body
I make this small offering for their resurrection:

Forgive me my sins.
Forgive me my sons.

Take me, instead.

BLOOD

I was eleven the first time I saw a girl bleed.
Between the boy's restroom and a storage bungalow,
we watched, in rapture, two girls begin to beat
one another. A single drop blossoming on a white
blouse. It didn't stop. Soon, it spread across their
pants, spilled onto the concrete beneath them,
one girl, the smaller girl, beaten so badly she
could not fight back and instead—her blouse
ripped open—covered herself, one hand over
her breasts, the other clutched into the black hair
of the girl who would not stop—the hollow pop
of her fists against cheek. I swear, I could smell
it, like rust in the air and as I walked back across
the blacktop, I felt it. Slowly, my stomach turned.
At home, I locked myself in the bathroom to vomit,
afraid to feel what between my legs grew swollen.

MEDITATIONS ON LEAVING

The first person to leave me
was my father. He took with him
my memories: hollow-boned

animals perched in his beard.
Flightless, in his back pocket,
the butterfly knife he gave me.

~

When you leave them, leave only what you can't carry.
Beneath a mattress, stacked in the medicine cabinet,
on a note left in a book resting on a dust-covered shelf
                              leave your memories.

~

The first time I made my mother cry,
            we sat at the dining room table. She
asked me to bring her a spoon. What
            I brought was a joke: the largest one
I could find: serving size to imply how
            much she ate. She left the room holding
her face in her moist hands. How hungry
            she must have been for an apology.
Because I did not show remorse my
            brothers beat me blue for what
I did not know: how easily
            I could hurt the first woman I loved.

~

Think better days. Think early. Think Saturday mornings. Cartoons. Roadtrips. Salsipuedes. Your father driving sunny Sunday summer afternoons through a trail of red taillights. Not the coming or going, but being stuck in it. The long goodbye. Think what you'd give for one more warm morning: the smell of your parents still in bed making
space   for you   between them.

～

When she didn't come home, I'd call
        her. Call her. Call her. Call her every
cruel name I could think of. Three a.m., I'd
        speed through the city angry, anxious,
to bring her back. This time I'd make
        her stay. Stay put. Stay true. Make her
say sorry for how much she'd hurt me.

～

It took years to pronounce it. But open-mouthed,
I'd tell any woman who'd listen I loved them.

        Y****** from the local Denny's who drank
        with me in a cheap hotel room after her shift.

        M**** who made me wait almost an entire
        year before we did it and she cried afterward.

        The nameless in a back alley, back seat, seated
        in an empty theater, in a park-side parking lot.

It didn't matter. All my pretty words unable
to say I never again wanted to be   alone.

~

Say sorry. Say please. Say it again. Again. Say it always. In perpetuity.

~

In another room, I can hear him open and close drawers. Imagine him stuffing clothes into a duffel bag: a pair of jeans, undershirts, and three polos. Briefs and socks on one end, toothbrush on the other. This is how little a man carries with him when he goes. A lesson I learn from my father. This is the end of the love story.

~

Soon, you'll stop believing in such things.

~

You act like you know.

But you don't know

how dark the years,

afterward, will become.

~

Sprawled lazily across the sofa I study the faces of mothers and potential fathers yelling at one another, the veins on their necks pulsing after each hate-filled word, while behind them on the screen a small child, too young to understand what's

happening, smiles brightly. Before Maury reveals the results—
the outcome of which I've already determined after an entire
summer spent watching TV—my dad comes into the room
to tell me he's leaving. Though I don't want to admit it, this
is the last time he'll leave. He is the father. He is not the father.
After the commercial break, everything is revealed to me.

      He is never coming back.

~

We pick up from the floor what's left.
Dirty clothes. Bottles. Cigarette smoke

choking the room. *This is the last time,*
you say. You no longer love me. I beg

you. I'm not embarrassed. I love oldies.
What I have to tell you, what I sing into

your ears is decades old. Tenderly, I say,
I will love you till the day I die. Outside

it's a fool moon. Don't leave me alone.
The night is beginning to cast shadows

over the city. The streetlights flicker on.
But you're not in love. When you leave,

you leave for good. Red-eyed, I watch
your broken taillight blink in the distance.

SPANISH MIDTERM

We gather in a park, four of us each
with forties in hand, among the spray-
painted tree trunks, our voices strained
against the nearby 710 freeway. Jacob
and Romeo, home from deployment,
recount stories of near-death in the darkness
of another world I can only imagine. Jorge,
a father in high school, tells us how last
night, over the phone, his girlfriend told
him he would be a father again and wanted
then, to say to her that she had dialed
the wrong number or hang up, because
he says, he may be too much a coward
to be twice a father at only twenty-one.
I have nothing to offer. Instead, I talk
of days in high school when we ditched
fifth period English and drove to Pedro
with pounds of carne asada and twelve
packs of Coronas, days when we knew
little except the city in which we lived.
As we drink, drink more, drink again,
I watch a dark hush begin to fill the 710,
fill the trees, watch it crawl over countless
cigarette butts, the tossed bottle of Cuervo,
the failed Spanish midterm resting beside
my foot, an exam some student dropped

on purpose, I suppose, because of the red
"F" on top, written with a carelessness
I can remember clearly because I too
have failed. Today, here with old friends
whose faces I barely recognize in the dim
light of dusk, I am filled with a darkness,
a desire, really, I suppose fills all four of us:
to carelessly, effortlessly, as it if were that
easy, to abandon all our failures on the floor.

ELEGY FOR WHAT ONCE SLEPT IN A CAGE

1.

After an entire week swimming near the shore,
        afraid of riptides, afraid more

of what lurked beneath sand-clouded waters, my older
        brothers, bored, would reluctantly

help me build sandcastles instead. Our backs blazed,
        skin peeling from our faces,

we built with our bare hands the homes we hoped
        we'd one day live in;

sad structures we made, wet-heavy and falling apart,
        until the sun hung low

on the horizon and the waves turned from vermillion
        into firewater, and we'd kick

over what we had made, pick up our sandy shirts
        and trek back home, four of us

laughing in the hour of odd-shaped shadows, our
        silhouettes growing across

the dirt road before us into surprising shapes,
        more like men than boys.

2.

Through the beach we tiptoed over broken glass and embers,
firecrackers popping off too close to our faces, watched
for the riders who could not tame their galloping horses,

passed the stone-cobbled road, passed the speakers playing loudly
from the outdoor bar, *Baby Got Back*, passed women who danced
bikini-clad on rooftops, passed men gathered in circles beneath them

who howled in slurred concoctions of English and Spanish for them
to take off their clothes, passed their worn bodies chewed up and spit
out by the sun, passed the German Shepherds whose mouths snapped

out for our bodies from long chains. We stopped, finally, as always
at the cage, hoping that the lion, asleep most days, would today
be awake and pace, as it sometimes did, back and forth, the low

grumble of its breath rising before it roared, the four of us in the front
row of a sideshow that had long been forgotten. Instead, we watched
the lion sleep, the flies settling to sate from its closed lids, their thirst.

3.

No one ever said the animal was beautiful because
it wasn't. It lay in the cage caked in dirt, the smell
of urine whisking through the air. But what we
had heard, from the man who fed and cared for it,
who sprayed it with a hose when the stench became
unbearable, was that the lion was tame. *Docíl* was
the word he had used. But watching its calculated
pace in a cage too small, its emaciated body stirring
beneath its fur, I knew this man, doing what he was
paid to do, was too easy with words, and wild or not
wild, I knew this animal did not belong here, knew too
that the boy who stood beside us did not belong here
either, alone, unattended, four of us made five, until
we walked away and said nothing—not one single word—
about the boy who, as we looked back, now crouched
beside the cage, his small hands curled around wrought
iron, beneath a small handmade sign, rusted over and
corroded by sea air, hanging above the cage door—a too-
easy warning I could not read or pronounce: *Cuidado*.

4.

Twenty-four years later I learn, from the paper, his name—
all the details in black and white. Jesse crouched beside
the cage, Jesse's arm slipped between the wrought iron bars,

Jesse's fingers first grazed, then pulled the whiskers of the lion,
which at that moment, had woken from its sleep. And because
the lion was, and always would be, an animal, it had no allegiance

to Jesse, to the boy who for two days that week, stood beside
the cage too afraid to approach it, and who one day, for reasons
no one knows, reached his arm inside and pulled back absence.

Not bone. Not muscle or sinew. Only blood. His cry emanating
from his throat, open so wide, so black, it swallowed all of us.

5.

A man ran to pick up   the boy
                                 held him   tightly in his   two arms

a father yelled   help   holding who
                                 had once been   his perfect boy who was

now   a bleeding boy   dismembered
                                 remember   how he pinched the elbow

to stop   the bleeding   how he
                                 cried and cursed   the open-mouthed crowd

that now gathered   cursed god
                                 who left this   to happen   cursed the lion

cursed   the boy's   body
                                 trembling   in blood   cursed the arm

forever asleep cursed   this pain
                                 the beast   breathing   cursed anger

for what had become   a body
                                 bleeding   from inside   its red cage.

6.

The men, because they didn't know what else to do,
circled the cage and held in their hands the weapons

they had found: broom sticks, bottles, and bar stools
and they began to jab the lion through the cage bars

and throw bottles at the animal, which became wild with
nowhere to go, and, cursing the lion, yelling to distract

it, other men, with what they had found, began to fish
out the arm that lay wet with saliva, covered with dirt,

and the arm that was without a body, without a will,
without a shoulder to turn it moved closer to the edge

of the cage, until someone grabbed the arm and held
it up in his hand. I felt then, because one does not

always know when to turn away, my brother's hand
cover my eyes, the pink of his palm turning the world

black, but still I could see it, moist and motionless,
and imagined then that the arm, if an arm could hope,

hoped to be held one last time and that the hand, if
a hand could wish, might wish to touch something

or someone it recognized, just as now my brother
held me in his arms to let me know I was not alone.

7.

The young boy's cry never stopped; it found somewhere
in the flesh-hardened folds of my ears—a place to live—
and on certain nights, asleep, or pretending to be asleep,
I would hear him cry out again, the boy's small voice, at first
faint, growing louder until it was my own voice I heard,
crying out in the night, feeling a brother's hand on my face
covering my eyes, as if he knew, in my dream, I was looking
at that which could not, maybe never, be unseen and I would
wake, his arm around me, his fingers running through my hair,
telling me in the dark to open my eyes so I'd no longer be afraid.

EL ESPOSO DE LA LLORONA
HABLA A LOS MUERTOS

She sleeps beneath my bed—body of loam, skin-smothered algae.
She sings the names of the women I've loved ungently. A lament:

Santa del daño. Santa del sufrimiento. Santa sagrada del dolor.

At the altar of what's been lost, I light a candle. My cold lips tremble.
Perdóname, dios. Forgive me for who I've been, for who I still am.

Pray not to god, but to those who've drowned in your dark, dark soul.

Amada. Soledad. Bella. Carin. Maya. Faustina. Marisol. Mi madre,
Rosalinda, mi primer amor. I hurt you all to ease my own suffering.

You prefer to speak to their ghosts. But confess to them your pecados.

I never wanted a son. Didn't want him to have my hands, my rotted
heart. When I told you I loved you, I fed you all my dark creatures.

This is no metaphor, no dream. To remember is your lifelong penance.

In the morning, I find on the floor your puddled footprints. Walk into
the waters of your memory—not baptized, not cleansed—unforgiven.

CONVERSATIONS WITH MY FATHER

In our silence, it dawns on me that I look nothing like my father. I imagine with his thin nose, pale skin, and white-peppered beard he would have ridden horseback alongside the conqueror Cortez and, because of my dark skin, would have killed me—a prophecy fulfilled—without a single word between us. Driving four hours quietly through the dark, for reasons I cannot explain, my father begins to tell me about his life: how at seven he crossed the Rio Grande on his uncle's shoulders, how he returned every summer to Coxcatlán to cut sugarcane, how at sixteen, without a license without citizenship, without a father, he drove from Brownsville to Chicago to make a new home with his family in a distant city.

~

After years of not speaking to one another, he's brought me here to show me what he's built with his bare hands at nearly sixty-five years old. Tells me how hard he's worked—months building frames and hanging drywall, painting wall after bedroom wall in bright colors—one for each of his sons, he says—rooms empty except for the bare mattresses. He lifts up his pant legs to show me his bandaged calves, varicose veins, he explains, that burst and bled, shows me his hands blistered red, the sharp scent of paint and paint remover stuck to his body. I try to understand everything my father has endured to make this, try to know how he's pained himself to erect another story above a house no one, in years, has set foot in, but I can't.

~

In an apartment on the corner of Primrose and Main we learned to live —my father, brother, and I—without my mother. I blamed him for her leaving. Every morning and every night and every hour in between, I hated how he worked so hard to make a home. When he'd wake at six to get ready, to make us breakfast, I would purposely never thank him. When he'd drop me off at school before going to work—hours I knew he'd spend in DTLA traffic—I'd ignore him when he told me he loved me. When he cooked us dinner after work, the only father I knew who cooked, who'd use all four burners to make carne asada, chuletas de puerco, arroz con pollo, who'd pick up the dishes afterward to wash them, work my father's father never did, I'd tell him I wasn't hungry.

One night he came into my room—the light from the hallway behind him making him a shadow. He sat beside me on my bed for a while and told me the worst thing he had heard in his life: *Your Mami doesn't want to be with me anymore*, and he began to cry. I reached out to hold him and felt his body shake. I held him like I know he would have held me, held him like a man would hold a son. I couldn't believe my father was crying, this man who I'd never seen cry before, and didn't see cry that night, because we sat and held one another in the darkness of what we couldn't understand. *I'm sorry, Papi*, I said to console us both.

DOMESTIC DISPUTE

Slowly, you joke, we're killing ourselves. We smoke
cigarettes on the front porch after the storm has passed,
observing the aftermath: the jacaranda that has leaned
precariously over our apartment has been dismembered
and sheets of tattered rooftop lie on the floor. Slowly,
last night's slurred words return:
fuck   bitch   puta   maricón
           the ever-loud cacophony
of our addiction, almost impossible to quit. At five a.m.
there are so few words in my mouth, all of them like wet
leaves. The dew on the grass gleams in sunlight.
Purple blossoms sweep across the sidewalks and streets.
Gently, you rest your hand on my thigh. I float my hand
across the small of your back. *I love you*, I say, though
the words come roughly. You say, *Me too*. Getting up
to go back inside and leave the world so dangerously
beautiful. The screen door behind us closes and closes
gently, as if it could shush away every bit of our agony.

EL ESPOSO DE LA LLORONA REZA

Padre mio, que está pero no se donde,
        he olvidado su nombre.

Venga a nosotros nuestra ruina—sus pecados
        los he hecho en mi casa

como los ha hecho usted desde el cielo
        —para los hombres

que abandonan o matan a sus hijos.
        Deme hoy sus migajas

de pan y la costra seca de su cuerpo.
        Perdóneme mis manos

arrugadas y mojadas. No me deje caer
        en su tumba y libéreme

de los caminos malos de los hombres
        enloquecidos por el poder.

Amén.

FALLING ASLEEP

A lemon drops from a tree
—half a heartbeat

The rattle of a neighbor's AC

—a car chokes on the early morning
—wiper blades cut through cool mist

The soft cries of my mother in her room

—who hasn't dreamt of her mother in months
—who hasn't dreamt of her dead brother in years

Nothing disappears, I'm convinced, but simply lingers

—the lamp turned off, eyes shut, and still, hints of light
—all the world asleep while I dream the flesh of ghosts

I tell myself, over and over: *Open your eyes*

—the tiny, womb-wet body of an unborn child sleeps in my palm
—my grandmother's rubs the sign of the cross along my forehead

Finally, silence, though I have feared this most of my life

—my body kicks, wildly, at the approaching shadows in the dark
—my eyelids twitch like the last breaths of an animal before dying

IV

PORTRAITS OF BEASTS

Alebrije

I learn first to kill in small ways. Ask the de-winged bee in the bottle, the dove with BB's lodged in its belly, ask the boy, hands behind back, why he eats the words on the floor. Ask him why he's so hungry.

Then this: from my father's belly, I'm spit out—horned, hooved, and halved. I give up prayer for prey I devour, bloodthirsty. I weave lyrics into all my lies. Listen: I can tell you any goddamn thing you want to hear. I love you. I love you. You, are the love of my life—this life I want to refuse.

Here, take it: this worm, this baby chick. Gusanito. Pollito. Tail tucked between my legs. Drink wine from my porous nipples. Come deeper. You have nothing to be afraid of. When you're ready and wanting, I'll tear you in half too.

Strange and Worried Animal

If not worried, restless. If not restless, hungry. If not hungry, striving only to please you in strange ways. Say *sit*, it lays down. Say *beg*, it rolls over. Say *play dead*, it licks from your palm—its tongue a wet pumice stone—to know what you taste like. Admit you are capable of loving what kills, easily. The prey brought to your feet, fur-matted and bone-crushed.

You offer in return your small favors: stroke beneath its bloody jaw, open space on the white sheets of your bed. Say *good boy. Good boy. Good job*. But this animal, white-toothed and obedient, is capable of clenching between its jaws—with four hundred and six pounds of pressure—your windpipe. Accept, before it squeezes the last intelligible word from your throat, you are just another animal. This beast you've loved, the one inside you, you are unable to tame.

Hombre-Lobo

Beaten and unable to breathe—no fight left—you flee. Run through the streets, across yards. Spread yourself like a shadow—on all fours—on the ground between two parked cars. Behind you, you hear grown men howl at the moon, hear bullets let loose from their muzzles. You take deep breaths, stilling the animal trapped in your chest, and drink the blood pooling in your mouth.

With only loose change and the leftover bits of tobacco from two long-ago-smoked cigarettes in your pocket, you walk back home still wanting something else to consume. Street signs blurred, your reflection stumbling past every window of every parked car, you want to break him. You try, again and again, until it's only your knuckles that feel broken.

In the land of the blind, you've become the one-eyed king. The streetlights, bent over as if in confession, won't let you forget. Not the precise hour she told you she no longer loved you, not the way she cried when she slept, not the way, for most of your life, you've been afraid of what lurks in the dark. The more of it there is, the less of yourself you see.

At home, in bed, head still throbbing, you close your eyes. Your feet hurt from crossing the city with only anger in your belly. You don't know what, for all these years, has kept you alive—even if barely. At night, you've feasted on what walks before you, weaker. How convenient, come morning, to say you've forgotten. You wash the blood from your body, from beneath your nails, panting over your open wounds. You tell yourself, *Beware the moon*. It's easier if there's something else to blame for the monster you've become.

Cannibal

The boy you used to be prays knee-deep in a river. *Por favor, dios, dame fuerza.* His body soaked and soft: belly rolls, boy breasts, nipples dark and erect.

From the shore wet with shadows you watch him, your prey. You hear his heart murmuring about the man he one day hopes to be. Hear too, your hunger: *[his body will feed you for a week]*.

You creep between the trees, run your tongue across your teeth, sharp with want. You must consume the last remnants of the boy who bleats in his sleep. *[gordo lloron niñita chion]*.

Wrap your mouth across his muffled sigh. Eat through the fleshy folds of his skin, eyes rolled back in ecstasy. There is no substitute for meat ground between your hungry bones. *[this is a necessary sacrifice]*.

Filicide

This morning, hunched over the bathroom sink, you brush, with every frayed bristle, the teeth chewing in the palm of your hand. Anxiously, your gums grind against themselves. You have been hungry every year of your life, though almost everything has been hard to swallow. For breakfast, you dismember each one of your sons on the cutting board, watch them squirm beneath the blade you've sharpened. Toss them into the frying pan, telling each one: this is what will finally make you a man. You set the table for one. Sip black coffee from your favorite mug. You won't eat a bite; not even a taste. Sometimes the best way to devour is to keep your mouth shut.

Suspect

This is not you, but your body forced to feign prayer. A curbside confession: *Forgive me officer, for I have sinned.* On bended knees, arms raised, hands reaching for what little you know of god, you assume the position. Cruciform. Know what you have always assumed: you are just one breath away from breathlessness. This is not you, but your body made brilliant in orbs of blue and red light. This is not you but your body. Shrouded in siren-call. This is not you but your body. Last words from your mouth unheard pleas, voice hoarse from begging before it's holed. Your heart, like a fist, trying to hold on. You and not your body, blocks away. Still-warm bread beneath your arm. A bottle of glue in your pocket to teach your daughter that what's broken can be mended.

Opossum

Instead of telling her you no longer love her, you play dead. Your body breathless. Your tongue hanging flaccid from your lips. Because you want to be culpable for little or absolutely nothing, you tell her it was not you, but your corpse, that slept with other women: eyes shut, body cold, your forearms X'ed innocently over your chest. The truth is, a dead thing loves no one. When you held her hands, when you fucked her in the park, when over the phone you told her you loved her, your words were maggots crawling from your mouth. The flesh-bodied beasts, dirt-blind, consuming the last bits of you that were left alive. All your little lies were methane seeping from your rotting corpse.

V

MORNING BREATH

A child is lost in the neighborhood. The child is me. The child is not me. I walk to the beach where a cackle of hyenas runs along the shore—their manes wild with sand and sea foam. They look for small dogs on which to feed. My dog went missing last week. Its name boils in their stomachs, indigestible. In the horizon, I see a hurricane approach: tides rolling over themselves. I walk home and fall asleep.

At night, a child with rotting flesh perches above my chest, as small as a bird fallen from its nest. The child drools green slaver on my face and it feels like I'm drowning. I'm dragged from bed by a woman, a ghost. In my bedroom, in the kitchen, in the bathroom too, we make love and the moon whispers across her skin: her body the deep purple of plums. When she speaks I cannot understand. I try to speak but am mouthless.

Some nights, deer sleep beside me. I dream of dead bodies. I dream I am a body that will soon die. I see everything before the dream goes dark. At night, the lights flicker. Eyes open. Eyes closed. They flicker. I am an expert of shadows. I am the feral cat outside bitching about desire. I am the dog howling incessantly at the moon. I try to scream but I'm afraid to wake the neighbors, who sleep, who are always sleeping, always asleep, forever asleep and snoring.

I wake for breakfast. I sit on a chair of bees. I crack my head against the wall and yolk drips to the floor. A spider crawls over my body. It is my own hand scratching an itch from the beginning of time. I eat dried toast and hear a child cry loudly. I smoke a pipe and watch the clouds rise from the back of my head. Blood oozes down the wall in rivulets thick as syrup. I cry into a cup and it tastes like the sea.

EL ESPOSO DE LA LLORONA
VISITA LA TUMBA DE SU MADRE

Madre, cuando desperté esta mañana sabía que usted estaba muerta.
Solo, que no estaba muerta. Estaba viva. Con los años, más pequeña

y frágil. Pero viva. Vete a buscar a tus hijos, me suplico. No están muertos;
han crecido. Tienen sus propios niños quienes juegan junto al río sin miedo.

Isabel, me explico, antes de dejarme preguntar. El nombre de tu hijo es Abel.
Usted recitó los nombres de sus bisnietos, pilando, del río, piedra tras

piedra sobre mis palmas, una para cada uno de ellos hasta que me ahogue.
Tanto el río como el cementerio, usted dijo, están repletos de piedras.

COMING HOME

I am trying to remember the exact pitch of my mother's
young voice as she cried out—*chicles, chicles*—earning
pennies in the Plaza Municipal. I am trying to remember
the sheen of my father's skin as he cut sugarcane, sweat

glowing on his darkened body, toiling from dawn til dusk.
So that now, I might take the gum from my mother's hand
and reach out for my father's wrist to take away his machete.
So that I can lead them across time, across land, to the house

they will build cinder block by block, and guide their walk
across the tile they will lay, square after square, and introduce
the children they will bear, boy after boy after boy after boy.
The only house they can afford to build on a dirt road three

tollbooths south of Tijuana. Or this: a simpler truth:
as a thirty-year-old man I'll return to do the work that must
be done. Retrieve, from behind the door, the broom to sweep
from the house lightweight blankets of dust, sweep up from

the floor the work of forgetting the termites have done, sweep
the memories hanging from ceiling corners like spider webs.
I'll sweep the last echoes of silence from what's been
abandoned: a child waiting for his parents to come back home.

QUAKER OATS

Today the bears came out again
and grizzled outside my window,

hungry. Cloaked in a red hood,
I began to dream of oatmeal—dry

and clumpy—like my mother made
on Sunday mornings before church,

where I prayed to a God I didn't
believe in six days out of the week,

and, never satisfied, I complained it
was too hot or too cold just to annoy

her and some Sundays, told her that
even a wild bear wouldn't eat her

oatmeal, and she would cry over
the pot making the oats just right

and I would eat them whole, barely
chewing, before she sent me outside

to play in the backyard more
an overgrown forest, where I'd fall

asleep beneath a tree and dream
of being eaten for such small sins.

TEETH NEVER SLEEP II

Clearing out what's lived beneath my mother's bed,
I find, in a felt-lined jewelry box, a chatter of teeth

that prattle in my palm. Though I can't be certain—
memory clouded by twenty years of bedside dust—

I remember once, one night, while my father slept
on the couch, my mother took out tooth after tooth

from the box and recited the names of my brothers
from whose mouths they came, arranging them on

her bed into mouths that had not spoken in years.
Just a boy, I saw this was a ritual only she knew,

imagined it was her, alone at night, who collected,
from beneath our pillows, the boys we would never

again resemble. The small animals culled from our
mouths by my father: a loose tooth tied to a doorknob

or clenched between needle-nose pliers. Our bones.
Huesos. Huesos. A word so soft it belies the pools

of blood we swallowed, each of us wanting to keep
in our mouths what we feared losing or becoming.

EL ESPOSO DE LA LLORONA
SE ENCUENTRA SOLO

Sin ti, sin tu cuerpo, no había nadie a quien culpar o magullar.
Tú no era una bruja, ni medusa, una traidora, ni puta o piruja.

Lo que te culpé por haber hecho, con tus conjuros y serpientes,
tus caracoles y la magia negra de tu sexo, me lo hice a mí mismo

con mis propias manos. Toda la culpa vive en mi boca, zumbiando,
un enjambre de moscas devorando mi lengua, mi última palabra mala.

FULL MOON

In the slow-cooling afternoons of summer
—unable to brush, unable to hammer—
my father took from my hands whatever tool
I held and grumbled, *Just go and play outside.*
What I did not tell him, what I couldn't tell
him, was that beyond our front porch, nearly
everything made me afraid: la tijereta, rear end
upright, legs undulating, its pincers poised
to seize the flesh of my fingers. Or, unearthed,
los niños de la tierra, their red-horned mouths
ready to inject venom, their bodies miniature
versions of Satan, a beast I was told cried out
before being killed, like a child—like a boy.
Outside, my mother would find me crying
and sit beside me on a bench that barely
held us both and begin to hum a soft song
whose name, even now, escapes me. I never
asked for meaning. Both of us staring at a full,
yellow moon, she would tell the story
of my birth at dawn. *You were born beneath
that light,* she would say before nestling her
head on my lap. *I'm tired, mi'jo.* The pains
she complained of, in her arms, shoulders,
and back, came from laboring to build
her children and mother a home, hammer
and chisel in hands as she chipped at the new

concrete ceiling. What I didn't tell her, what
I couldn't tell her—watching the small particles
of concrete fill in the wrinkles around her eyes,
the wrinkles around her mouth, noticing how
in a few hours she had aged—is that I'd learned
she would not live forever. Nothing made me
more afraid. And I would begin to comb my hands
through her hair, from the top of her scalp down
to the bottom of each strand graying in moonlight,
the way she had taught me. This way, to keep us.

I SMOKE MY LAST CIGARETTE WHILE ANDRÉS MONTOYA PREACHES TO THE WILLOW TREE

When the phone rings, he tells me, *God is calling.*
Neither of us answers. Beneath a willow tree, half-

drunk at 2:45 p.m., I take inventory of the slow day:
a pit bull gnashing after the schoolchildren; the boy,

porch-ridden until his parents get off work at six,
who sharpens a stick on the sidewalk; the man who

pushes a shopping cart, black-lunged and bloated,
through the intersection. *I have to give up,* I tell him.

Andrés responds: *God's love is everlasting.* I say,
This is my last smoke. I'm making myself feel sick.

Jesus, were he alive today, he says, *would have no
home.* Slowly, I inhale and every breath kills me: like

gravel in my chest, my body begging. *We die with
only our bad habits,* he whispers, *and loving what*

kills us is the cruelest trick the Devil ever played.
In the kingdom of this city I have begun to hate,

I watch the light being choked from the neon sky.
The breeze passing through the leaves turns them

beautifully iridescent. It's enough to make me cry.
I confess, *everything in this city will soon break us.*

Andrés begins to recite a prayer that sounds faintly familiar. When I can no longer hear him, I say, *Amen.*

EL ESPOSO DE LA LLORONA TIENE UNA MIRADA DE ESPERANZA

Después de la oscuridad de mi luto,
veo mi reflejo refractado en el agua.

ANTIPODE

In front of wood-warped shack in Patagonia stands a mule. In its eye you see something wet, stooped beneath the rain —the saddest creature you'll ever see. Say it's not the mule, but your mother standing there, suitcase in hand, waiting by the train tracks that long ago corroded. Here, the ocean cares little what you do with your life, and the skies, purple plumed in white, are indifferent, always cold. Tell her what you know. This land will never be good to her. Remind her how once she ripped open a pomegranate and piled seed after seed into your palm until you forgot your hunger. That was years ago. Tell yourself what you know. Tomorrow will be the best day for your departure to a city across the world. The rains will soon stop. Finally, the soil will be soft enough to embrace her.

CAGES

Six years I won't love a woman. I don't let myself. I sit, instead, once a week in a circle of mostly men and attempt to name the wild beasts running through my blood. Years ago, I threw the boy I once was in the cage. Locked the cage door behind me. Watched what happened when the feeding began. The snarl and bark, an appetite whetted, and wanting first to eat my teeth.

I don't know who I am without fist or knuckle. I am no one without the bottle and what it brings in blood. I wander the streets looking for what will sate me. Wait, patiently, for what comes walking my way. When I finally love someone, I am only prey. When she touches me, I am a charm of finches, a flight of swallows, afraid of the overhead shadow. My body is a herd jumping back from the river's edge, afraid of what breathes in muddy waters. I pray I won't let loose what lurks inside. The beasts are hungry for my return: the king of animalia.

MEDITATIONS ON LOSS

My mother calls out the names of my brothers
      Juan   Javier   Rene
          until   finally
she picks my name: a penny in a purse full of change.

~

Here   a spackled-over hole from where a picture once hung.
Here   dust passing through a sliver of light from open curtains.

~

I fill box after box, empty room after room:
from each house I take what I can't live without.

      I ask again and again what city we now live in.
      I wonder, where my brothers have moved.

~

Years later, you've failed a test. After school, at sunset, you watch three brothers play basketball with their dad. Their laughter echoes, bounces through the corridors. Soon, they become oversized shadows. There are no rules: this is for sheer pleasure. You walk across the blacktop not wanting to go home. Your body shudders—something you've carried around all these years but can no longer bear to hold in.

~

From the bar to the bedroom, from the bedroom to the bar,
I prefer walking and waking in the dark. Lights off, drunk,
I wade through the glass-bodied fishes open-mouthed
on the floor, struggling for the last gasp of fresh air.

～

*Curled up beside you, death rubs your belly. Fucking is lament.
Because you need convincing, it assures you. Tells you you're
a good lay, tells you any goddamn thing you want to hear.*

～

*You've lit candles. You've left flowers on doorsteps
and so many handwritten letters. Signed. Sealed.*

*But never delivered. This isn't love. Don't be fooled.
This is how you leave them. This is how you grieve.*

～

The night my girlfriend tells my mother I beat her,
I feel betrayed. This was a secret we kept between us.
That night, I was no longer my mother's loving son.

～

Her hand, more wrinkled, moves across my hand.
I've never known such warmth. On a hospital bed,
the black-and-white monitor behind her displays her

    bleeding heart: an artery seeping blood into her lungs.
       In pain, she says, *Estoy tomando mis vacaciones*:
      a joke meant to ease our suffering. I don't laugh.
       In a few days my grandmother will be dead.

∼

The first women I love belong to others. When they kiss my lips,
they tell me I'm beautiful. Tell me I am beautiful *to* them. Until
it hurts too much.   *Now you can't love a woman without*
drinks in you. You claim not to have a problem. Your broken lies
            betray you.

∼

She tells me, when for months, for years, I've grieved,
     The baby wasn't yours. Let it go.

Even the mourning I've carried in my arms
      does not belong to me.

∼

The summer you first drink whiskey the bottle is still
in its box. In an empty house, in a new city, it tingles
through your body. What's empty you fill until
you are a different version of yourself.

∼

I have of hers a gold necklace she gave me at birth.

    You lost it drunk. Snapped off your neck in a fight.

From her house, after her death, I took a nail crucifix.

    You said you'd never lose what mattered most.

I can't seem to remember the way she loved me.

    In a parking lot, bleeding, you go looking for it.

Father, for so many years I've tried to forgive you.

    When he's dead, you'll have only yourself to hate.

I never wanted to be this kind of animal.

    Once you got your first taste, you craved the blood.

My mother tells me I'll die alone with no one left.

    God willing, you won't bear the beasts not yet named.

NOTES

The epigraph at the beginning of the collection is from Fernando Pessoa's collection *The Book of Disquiet*.

"Antipode I" and "Antipode II" were inspired by the documentary film, ¡*Vivan las Antípodas!* and the dramatic film, *La Sirga*, respectively.

"Bones" was inspired by the work of poet Etheridge Knight, specifically the poem, "The Bones of My Father."

"Rinconcito" uses lines from the Ramón Ayala song, "Un Rinconcito en el Cielo" and begins with lines taken from the song "Stay in My Corner" by The Dells.

"Self-Portraits of a Man as Beast: Ablutions" begins with an epigraph from Gloria Anzaldúa's *Borderlands/La Frontera: The New Mestiza*.

"Giving It" was inspired by Vievee Francis' poem "Taking It" in her collection, *Forest Primeval*.

"Meditations on Leaving" and "Meditations on Loss" were inspired by the work of Ocean Vuong.

"Elegy for What Once Slept in a Cage" is inspired by true events that took place on Saturday, June 27th, 1992. The author was approximately nine years old.

"Portraits of a Beast: Hombre-Lobo" uses a line from the film *An American Werewolf in London*.